GW00392076

A GUIDE TO

THE WEST DORSET

COUNTRYSIDE

A GUIDE TO

THE WEST DORSET COUNTRYSIDE

Chris Jesty

Weather vane at Bothenhampton

Dovecote Press

Uniform with this volume:
"A Guide to the Isle of Purbeck"

———————

First published in 1986 by
The Dovecote Press Ltd, Stanbridge, Wimborne, Dorset

ISBN O 946159 36 X

Printed in Great Britain by Biddles Ltd, Guildford, Surrey,

———————

The maps in this book are based upon the Ordnance Survey maps
with the permission of the Controller of H.M. Stationery Office.

CONTENTS

KEY TO THE MAPS

	Recommended for driving	Recommended for walking	Linking route for walkers
Main road	▬▬▬▬		
Minor metalled road	══════	════════	
Unmetalled road or track	══════	════════	=:=:=:=:=:=
Path		‑ ‑ ‑ ‑ ‑ ‑	‑·‑·‑·‑·‑
No visible path (not used along the beach)			....

Parking place	▬▪▬
Public convenience	PC
Highest point of hill	△
Attractive traditional buildings	▨
Unattractive or modern buildings	▥
Heath	\ \ / / /
Slopes (thick ends at the top)	! ! ! ! ! !
Water	∴∴∴

Lettering

HILLS

TOWNS, VILLAGES AND HAMLETS

Water features

Other features

Routes recommended for walking are of scenic interest, and not usually muddy in the summer.

TRAVELOGUE — The A 35 from Dorchester to Bridport

Dorchester is a Roman town, and the road leading out of it is a Roman road. When you are clear of the built-up area you can see on the left Maiden Castle, the best-preserved and best-known hill fort in Britain. The pillar on the skyline is the Hardy Monument.

Just past the first crossroads you pass close to a fine round barrow with bushes growing out of it.

After about a mile the main road bends round to the left, while the line of the Roman road is taken up by a minor road going straight on. As you descend the next hill you can see old strip lynchets or cultivation terraces in the field straight ahead.

The road now enters the attractive village of Winterbourne Abbas, many of whose cottages are built of alternating layers of flint and stone. The stream running along the side of the road is the Winterborne, so called because it only flows in the winter.

As you leave the village look out for a bronze age stone circle called the Nine Stones in a wood on the left. Just past here is a lodge house which stands at a former entrance to the mansion of Bridehead.

Opposite the next turning on the right is the Poor Lot group of round barrows.

The road now straightens out, and a neolithic bank barrow is visible on the skyline to the left of the road. This is an extra long "long barrow", and marks the western terminus of the string of round barrows on the Dorset Ridgeway. There are two round barrows aligned with the bank barrow to the right of it.

The road then descends to a col, and rises to its highest point, 700 feet above sea level. From the layby on the left you can see across Lyme Bay to Beer Head and, on a clear day, to Dartmoor.

From the end of the dual carriageway Eggardon Hill is visible on the right; and as you pass the R.A.C. telephone the view opens up and all the hills and valleys of West Dorset are laid out before you. From here onwards it's downhill most of the way.

PHYSICAL FEATURES OF WEST DORSET

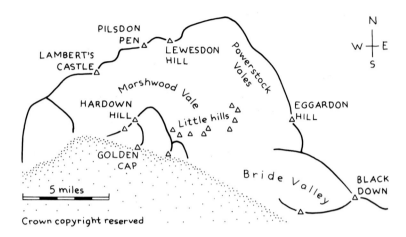

Crown copyright reserved

West Dorset consists of two concentric horseshoe-shaped ridges centred on the valley of the little River Winniford. Between the two ridges is the Marshwood Vale. At the eastern end of the Marshwood Vale is a string of little hills running roughly east-west; and north-east of here is the Powerstock Vales, an area characterised by deeply incised valleys and sunken lanes.

The western limb of the inner horseshoe divides at Hardown Hill into two ridges, one going over Chardown Hill to the sea, and the other going over Langdon Hill to Golden Cap. Between these two ridges is the valley of St Gabriel's Water. For many years this valley has been shown as a ridge on the Quarter Inch map.

The eastern limb of the inner horseshoe also divides into two, but here the eastern ridge is lower and less significant than the western. The valley between these two ridges is drained by a stream called the Eype.

The presence of so many ridges truncated by the sea gives rise to striking coastal scenery, which is enhanced by the complex geology of the region; and there is no better place from which to view this scenery than Devonshire Head.

DEVONSHIRE HEAD

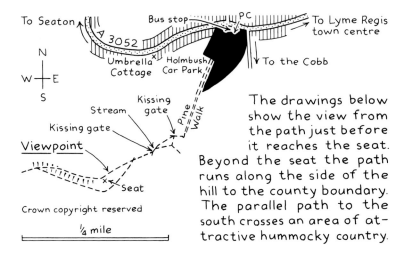

The drawings below show the view from the path just before it reaches the seat. Beyond the seat the path runs along the side of the hill to the county boundary. The parallel path to the south crosses an area of attractive hummocky country.

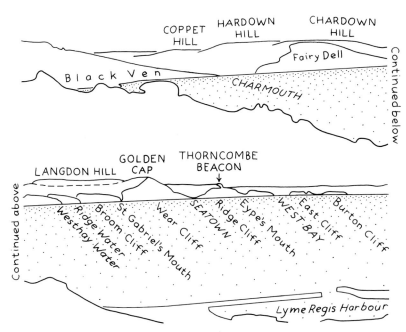

Chapter 2
TIMBER HILL

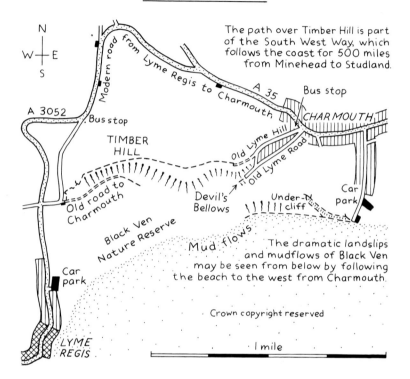

The path over Timber Hill is part of the South West Way, which follows the coast for 500 miles from Minehead to Studland.

The dramatic landslips and mudflows of Black Ven may be seen from below by following the beach to the west from Charmouth.

1 mile

Ascent from Lyme Regis

This route has the advantage of easy parking, but because the best scenery is on the Charmouth side of the hill, it is worth going some distance beyond the highest point before returning.

The path leaves the old road to Charmouth just past the gate, and ascends the hillside by some well-made steps through tall beech trees. Then it wanders on through a sycamore wood and comes to a T-junction. Just before the junction the path passes through an area of badger setts. These will have been passed on from generation to generation for hundreds of years. To get some idea of the length of the tunnels, look at the amount of earth piled up outside their entrances.

Turn right at the junction. The path bears left along the edge of the wood, and then bears right and enters a sunken stretch that used to be muddy but is now well-maintained. The path bends left and immediately right. Then there follows a stretch of cliff-top path that is unsurpassed anywhere for scenic beauty.

The first section is fenced on the left, and on the right looks down on an undercliff that is covered in bracken and dotted with a wide variety of shrubs. The sea is nearly 600 feet below and over 600 yards away.

The second section is unfenced. The undercliff is less beautiful than in the first section, but more spectacular. A whole hillside is on the move. At first cracks appear in the grass at the top of the cliff. Then the ground is split into great blocks which slide slowly down the hillside. Farther down, uprooted gorse bushes are strewn around, and at the foot of the cliff mud flows can be seen pushing their way out to sea.

Just beyond the boundary hedge there is a striking view down a gully on the right.

Ascent from Charmouth

On maps published before about 1925, both Old Lyme Hill and Old Lyme Road are shown joining up with the old road to the west, but the linking sections have completely disappeared. The latest Ordnance Survey maps show a public footpath going west from the end of Old Lyme Road, but now this too has gone. The last stretch of road is grass-covered, but its course is easy to follow. It passes through a deep cutting called the Devil's Bellows, and then it plunges over a cliff.

Nowadays, anyone walking from Charmouth to Lyme Regis should take the upper road (Old Lyme Hill). This ends in quite a different way. When the last house is reached the modern road surface gives way to the rough stony surface of the old road. The very last stretch is an impenetrable tangle of vegetation. To avoid this the footpath sidesteps to the right. Then it comes out onto the clifftop, and you can look across the vast empty space that was once crossed by the road.

Chapter 3

CHARDOWN HILL

The road from Bridport to Lyme Regis passes between two hills that are similar both in name and in appearance. Hardown Hill is on the right, and Chardown Hill is on the left. Hardown Hill descends steeply in all directions, but

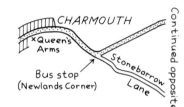

Continued opposite

Chardown Hill extends a long ridge to the south-west which ends dramatically five hundred feet above the sea. This ridge is known as Stonebarrow Hill, and it may be approached by car from Charmouth along a steep and narrow lane. There is ample provision for car parking along the ridge, and the National Trust has a shop here in the summer.

The advantage of Stonebarrow Hill over Timber Hill, Golden Cap and Thorncombe Beacon is that the cliff-top can be reached by a short level walk from the car park. From the west end of the car park take the path along the ridge to the point marked "viewpoint" on the map. From here you get a bird's eye view of that wild and enchanting stretch of undercliff that is known as the Fairy Dell. Rabbits are plentiful in the undergrowth, kestrels hang suspended in mid-air, and if you come early in the morning you are likely to see a deer or two. This is a place to return to time and time again.

From the viewpoint paths follow the cliff-top in both directions. From the path to the east there are a number of alternative ways back to the car park.

Another interesting walk starts at the east end of the car park. Go through the little wooden gate and take the path (signposted to St Gabriels) that goes diagonally down the hill. The path curves round to the left, runs along the top of an area of gorse and bracken, and crosses over a peaceful valley that runs down to the sea. It then goes through a little wooden

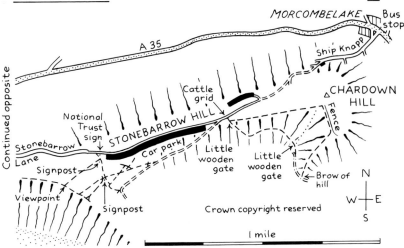

gate and joins a track. If the track is too muddy, go back through the little gate and climb the hillside. Otherwise, keep on the track until you come to the brow of the hill, and then take a path on the left that climbs up the ridge. Turn left when you reach the fence, and left again at the corner of the field. You are now close to the highest point on Chardown Hill, and the car park is straight ahead.

<u>The Queen's Arms</u> at Charmouth was patronised by Queen Catherine of Aragon in 1501 and by King Charles II in 1651. The building is much older than it appears to be from the outside, and it contains many fifteenth-century features including a window, a doorway and a fireplace.

<u>Cain's Folly</u> was a group of trees that were planted on the cliff-top and gradually disappeared as the cliffs were worn away. Now all that remains is a name on the Ordnance Survey map.

   Before 1820 the main road from Morcombelake to Charmouth passed over Stonebarrow Hill.

Chapter 4
HARDOWN HILL

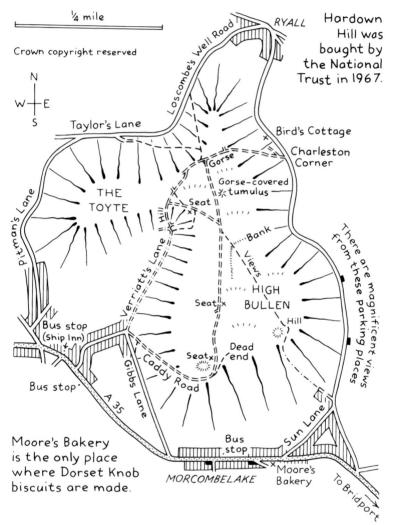

¼ mile

Hardown Hill was bought by the National Trust in 1967.

N
W—E
S

RYALL

Loscombe's Well Road

Taylor's Lane

Bird's Cottage

Charleston Corner

Gorse

Gorse-covered tumulus

THE TOYTE

Pitman's Lane

Seat

Bank

Verriatt's Lane Hill

Views

HIGH BULLEN

Hill

Seat

There are magnificent views from these parking places

Bus stop (Ship Inn)

Seat

Dead end

Gibbs Lane

Caddy Road

Seat

Bus stop

A 35

Bus stop

Sun Lane

MORCOMBELAKE

Moore's Bakery

To Bridport

Moore's Bakery is the only place where Dorset Knob biscuits are made.

Hardown Hill is so beautiful there really ought to be a society for the preservation of it. In fact there is; and it's volunteers from the Hardown Preservation Society who keep the paths in such good condition.

Before I came to live in this area I stayed at Bird's Cottage in Ryall. It was an interesting old cottage, stepped up the hillside, with glorious views over the valley of the River Winniford. I only had to go a few yards along the lane and up a rough track between high gorse bushes, and I was on Hardown Hill.

The summit of Hardown is covered with bell heather and dwarf gorse; and the track that crosses the plateau from north to south makes a delightful walk. It passes a gorse-covered tumulus on the left, and then it passes an L-shaped bank, which marks the parish boundary between Whitechurch Canonicorum and Chideock. A narrow path crosses the bank and carries on over High Bullen to the edge of the plateau.

The main track continues southwards, passing a seat on the left. Langdon Hill and Golden Cap are now visible ahead. Behind the next seat is an interesting area of disused quarries. The bushes growing here that look like gorse but have no spines are broom.

A quarter of a mile to the north is a third seat. It looks across at Chardown Hill, which is seen framed in a valley with the sea on either side.

When travelling by bus it is best to alight at the Ship Inn, Morcombelake, and ascend the hill by the sunken track called Caddy Road. The routes from Taylor's Lane and Loscombe's Well Road are also recommended, but the route from the south-east has a muddy patch and is slightly overgrown.

Pines on Hardown Hill

Chapter 5

GOLDEN CAP

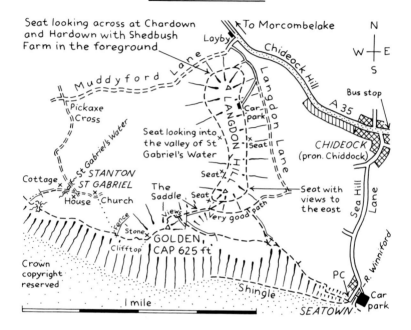

Seat looking across at Chardown and Hardown with Shedbush Farm in the foreground

To Morcombelake

Layby

Chideock Hill

N W+E S

M u d d y f o r d

Langdon Lane

Pickaxe Cross

Bus stop

A 35

St Gabriel's Water

Car park

LANGDON HILL

Langdon Lane

CHIDEOCK (pron. Chiddock)

Seat looking into the valley of St Gabriel's Water

Seat

Cottage

STANTON ST GABRIEL

House   Church

Seat

The Saddle   Seat

Seat with views to the east

Sea Hill Lane

Crown copyright reserved

Fence

Stone

views

very good path

Clifftop

GOLDEN CAP 625 ft

R. Winniford

PC

1 mile

Shingle

SEATOWN

Car park

Ascent from the A 35

At 625 feet, or 191 metres, Golden Cap is the highest point on the south coast of England. The easiest route of ascent is from the car park on Langdon Hill. A broad, well-surfaced path follows a contour all the way round the hill, so maintaining a level course through the steeply sloping woodland. There are no fewer than six seats in the course of the circuit, and these are generally situated where there are gaps in the trees.

From the far end of the circular walk a signposted path leads down to the Saddle and up to Golden Cap. As it climbs through the gorse there are beautiful views on the right.

An alternative route is to continue along Langdon Lane when the road leaves for the car park, and then turn right at the T-junction into Pettycrate Lane.

Ascent from Seatown

Despite its name, Seatown is a tiny hamlet; and the River Winniford, which flows through it, is not a river, but a small stream. Sometimes the stream runs into the sea, but usually it sinks into the pebbles a short distance inland.

The path leaves from the end of the road. For 200 yards it runs along the undercliff. Then it follows the cliff-top for a quarter of a mile and crosses a wide open space. At the foot of Golden Cap it bears right and joins the route from Langdon Hill.

Ascent from St Gabriel's

The village of Stanton St Gabriel consists of no more than a house, a cottage and a ruined church. The shortest route goes past the church and cuts across to the cliff-top, but a more interesting route passes St Gabriel's Cottage and joins the coast path farther west.

After crossing St Gabriel's Water turn right onto a path, and then right again onto a rough track. Close to the junction is a well-preserved sheep wash. The track leads to a little corner of Dorset that hasn't changed for centuries. Close to the stream, and looking out over a meadow, is a perfect little thatched cottage.

Keep straight on to the cliff-top and turn left. From the coast path there is a view of the cottage in its rural setting, and farther on, just before the fence, there is a spectacular view of the steep south face of Golden Cap.

The Summit

At the north-eastern end of the summit plateau is an Ordnance Survey column. This is linked by a well-worn path to a stone plaque erected in 1978 in memory of Lord Antrim, the Chairman of the National Trust. On the back of the stone is the internal mould of part of an enormous ammonite.

Shedbush Farm under snow (as seen from Langdon Hill)

Looking west from Golden Cap

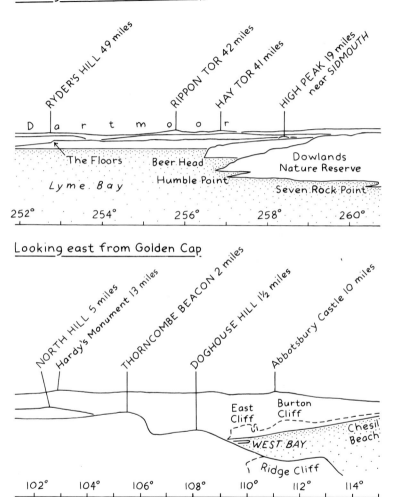

RYDER'S HILL 49 miles

RIPPON TOR 42 miles

HAY TOR 41 miles

HIGH PEAK 19 miles near SIDMOUTH

D a r t m o o r

The Floors

Beer Head

Humble Point

Dowlands Nature Reserve

Seven Rock Point

Lyme Bay

252°   254°   256°   258°   260°

Looking east from Golden Cap

NORTH HILL 5 miles

Hardy's Monument 13 miles

THORNCOMBE BEACON 2 miles

DOGHOUSE HILL 1½ miles

Abbotsbury Castle 10 miles

East Cliff   Burton Cliff

Chesil Beach

WEST BAY

Ridge Cliff

102°   104°   106°   108°   110°   112°   114°

Conclusion According to Bennet Copplestone's novel, the Treasure of Golden Cap lies under the flagstones of St Gabriel's church, but the real treasure of Golden Cap is its gorse-covered slopes, its sandstone cliffs and its delectable views of the Dorset countryside.

Chapter 6
QUARRY HILL

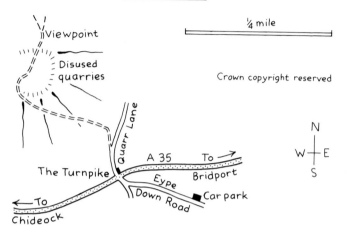

Quarry Hill is the continuation of the ridge from Thorncombe Beacon over Eype Down, but although Eype Down is predominantly bracken, Quarry Hill is covered in grass.

The crossroads at the highest point on the road from Bridport to Chideock is locally known as the Turnpike, and there is a Turnpike Cottage near by. Leave the junction by a narrow metalled road heading north, and in a hundred yards bear left onto an unsurfaced track. The parish boundary follows the track, indicating that it is older than the metalled road.

Go through a gate and turn left uphill, following the right-hand side of a fence. As the track bends round to the right it passes through a fascinating area of little hillocks, the result of quarrying. Like Allington Hill and Sloes Hill, Quarry Hill is capped with Oolitic Limestone. This is the stone found in the Cotswolds, and it explains the resemblance of many Dorset buildings to those of the Cotswolds.

When the track becomes a path the hillocks end, and there are good views to the east.

EYPE DOWN

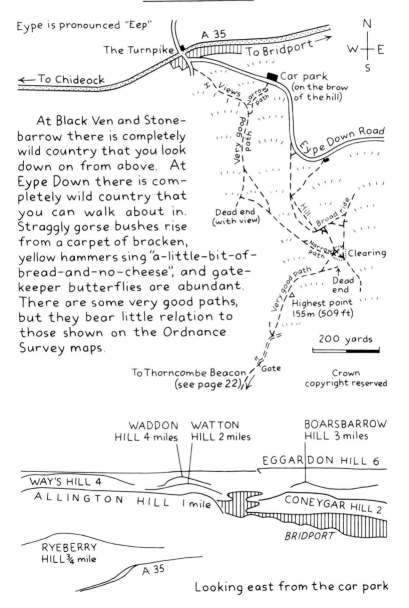

Eype is pronounced "Eep"

The Turnpike

A 35

To Bridport

N
W—E
S

← To Chideock

Car park
(on the brow
of the hill)

Views

Narrow path

Very good path

Eype Down Road

At Black Ven and Stone-barrow there is completely wild country that you look down on from above. At Eype Down there is com-pletely wild country that you can walk about in. Straggly gorse bushes rise from a carpet of bracken, yellow hammers sing "a-little-bit-of-bread-and-no-cheese", and gate-keeper butterflies are abundant. There are some very good paths, but they bear little relation to those shown on the Ordnance Survey maps.

Dead end
(with view)

Hill

Broad ride

Narrow path

Clearing

Very good path

Dead end

Highest point
155m (509 ft)

200 yards

To Thorncombe Beacon
(see page 22)

Gate

WADDON
HILL 4 miles

WATTON
HILL 2 miles

BOARSBARROW
HILL 3 miles

EGGARDON HILL 6

WAY'S HILL 4

ALLINGTON HILL 1 mile

CONEYGAR HILL 2

BRIDPORT

RYEBERRY
HILL ¾ mile

A 35

Looking east from the car park

Chapter 8

THORNCOMBE BEACON

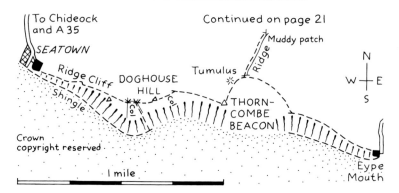

Continued on page 21

Ascent from Eype Down (continued from the map on page 21). This route has the advantage of starting 300 feet higher than the other two, but it has the disadvantage of a muddy patch by the gate at the south end of Eype Down. Beyond the gate the path follows the ridge to Thorncombe Beacon.

Descent   Keep right of the tumulus, and leave the area by a stile consisting of three horizontal planks.

Ascent from Seatown   The path leaves from the car park and follows the cliff-top. On the way up there is a delightful view of Seatown with Golden Cap and Langdon Hill behind it.

At the top of Ridge Cliff the path leaves the cliff-top and makes for a gap in the fence. From the summit of Doghouse Hill you can see how the cliffs of Thorncombe Beacon are made up of different layers. At the top is the Bridport Sands with its horizontal calcareous bands. Lower down is another sandy layer, the Thorncombe Sands, which is a little less distinct. Between the two is the Down Cliff Clay, and below the Thorncombe Sands is the Down Cliff Sands.

Beyond Doghouse Hill the route follows a lovely downland ridge to a little col and then carries on to Thorncombe Beacon.

Descent   From the east side of the valley separating Doghouse Hill from Ridge Cliff, a steep grassy path descends to the beach. It starts off by following traces of an old fence and is recommended to lovers of solitude.

This route is not recommended for ascent because of the difficulty of finding the path from the beach.

Ascent from Eype Mouth   The path leaves from the car park, which is at the end of the road. From the top of the first rise you can see Down House Farm ahead of you at the foot of Eype Down. This is where R.C. Sherriff the playwright lived. In 1966 he gave the farm to the National Trust, along with this stretch of coastline.

The cliff-top route to Thorncombe Beacon involves a considerable descent and re-ascent, but this can be avoided by making a detour to the right.

The Summit   On the highest point is a seat facing the sea, and surrounded by a wooden fence. The altitude is 515 feet, or 157 metres. 200 yards north of the summit is a fine bracken-covered tumulus.

Looking north from Thorncombe Beacon

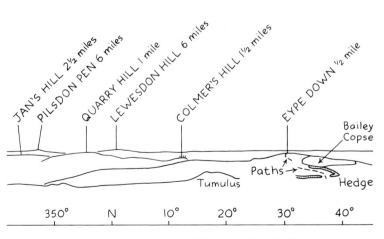

Looking east is a lovely view of the undercliff.

Chapter 9

WEST BAY

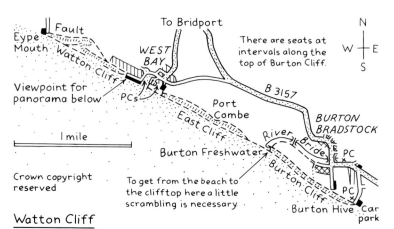

There are seats at
intervals along the
top of Burton Cliff.

To get from the beach to
the clifftop here a little
scrambling is necessary.

Watton Cliff

If you cut a very thin slice of cake the thin end of the
slice will tend to crumble. The same thing happens when a
geological fault cuts across the coastline at a small angle,
and this phenomenon may be observed from the top of
Watton Cliff.

When walking from West Bay to Eype Mouth bear right
at the end of the houses. The first sign of the fault is a
little valley running along the left-hand side of the path.
Farther on the path follows the top of a cliff. This cliff
makes an angle of 17° with the coastline, and marks the
line of the Eype Mouth Fault. The point where the cliff
turns southward is called Fault Corner.

Looking west from West Bay

The Floors is a cliff between
Exmouth and Budleigh Salterton

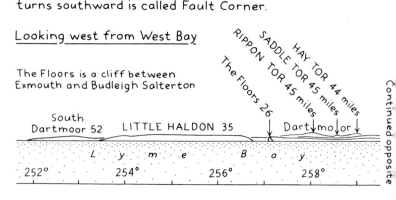

Continued opposite

East Cliff

The cliff between West Bay and Burton Freshwater differs from those further west in being vertical, but East Cliff is more than a vertical wall: it is a piece of natural architecture, worthy of comparison with any castle or cathedral. Where there has been a recent cliff fall, the face is smooth. Then the weaker layers are steadily eroded away leaving a series of horizontal calcareous bands that are closer together near the top. The cliff is composed of a beautiful golden yellow rock called the Bridport Sands; and it has the additional advantage of being easily accessible.

East Cliff is recognisable in distant views by the dramatic hanging valley of Port Combe, three-fifths of the way along. There is no way down to the beach here.

Burton Cliff

Burton Cliff is similar to East Cliff in character, except that there is a thin layer of Inferior Oolite above the Bridport Sands, and, where the cliff is highest, there is a layer of Fuller's Earth above the oolite. The Inferior Oolite is the familiar "Cotswold" building stone, and the Fuller's Earth is a grey earth-like rock.

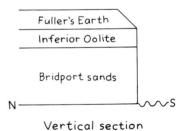

Vertical section

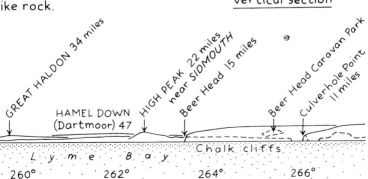

Chapter 10

CHESIL BEACH

Cogden Beach to West Bexington

From Cogden Car Park the coast path passes between the reed beds of Burton Mere and the vast shingle bank of the Chesil Beach. The reed beds are the haunt of water rails.

← To Burton Bradstock

Cogden Beach (part of Chesil Beach)

Cogden Car Park

Burton Mere (reed beds)

Continued opposite

On the seaward side of the beach the movement of the pebbles by the waves makes it impossible for anything to grow, but on the landward side there are isolated clumps of sea kale (a cabbage-like plant) and occasional clumps of samphire. In the valley separating the beach from the mainland there are masses and masses of thrift. Another plant that grows here is the yellow horned-poppy, which has longer seedpods than any other British plant.

Between Burton Mere and Swyre Mere the path is covered by shingle. It is a long uphill walk to the crest from here.

Swyre Mere is shown on the Landranger map, but not on the Pathfinder. Both maps are correct, because the lake completely dries up in the summer, and the land is used as pasture. The reedbeds to the east of Swyre Mere are a nature reserve managed by the Dorset Naturalists' Trust. At West Bexington there is a car park which slopes up to the top of the beach.

West Bexington to Abbotsbury

Throughout most of its length the Chesil Beach rises from the land before descending to the sea, but there is a stretch to the east of West Bexington where the land is higher and where the beach descends straight to the sea. Alexanders, mallow and thrift grow in this area, and farther east, tamarisk bushes are much in evidence.

A mile to the east of Burton Bradstock the West Dorset coast undergoes a transformation. From here onwards there are no high cliffs, no deep valleys, just miles and miles of pebbles. The appeal of the Chesil Beach lies not in grandeur or variety, but in simplicity.

The walk along Limekiln Hill is recommended both for its views and for its wild flowers. The land is owned by the National Trust.

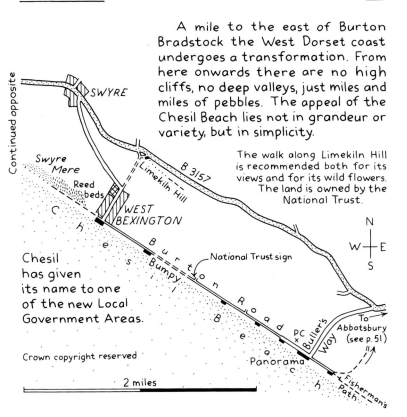

Continued opposite

SWYRE

Swyre Mere

Reed beds

B 3157

Limekiln Hill

WEST BEXINGTON

Chesil has given its name to one of the new Local Government Areas.

N
W — E
S

Chesil Beach

Burton Bumpy Road

National Trust sign

Buller's Way

To Abbotsbury (see p. 51)

PC

Panorama

Fisherman's Path

Crown copyright reserved

2 miles

At the junction of Burton Road and Buller's Way there is a panorama in which High Peak is identified as Start Point. Start Point is not visible from this altitude because of the curvature of the earth, but it can be seen from Hardy's Monument.

From the end of the road the Fisherman's Path continues through the reedbeds. Then it steps across to the right and carries on between the reedbeds and the Chesil Beach. Here sea peas and sea campions grow on the landward side of the beach. The path ends at the row of concrete blocks called the Dragon's Teeth. Beyond this point the Chesil Beach is separated from the mainland by the long tidal lagoon known as the Fleet.

Chapter II

LAMBERT'S CASTLE

Lambert's Castle is named after King Lambert, who is better known as King Canute.

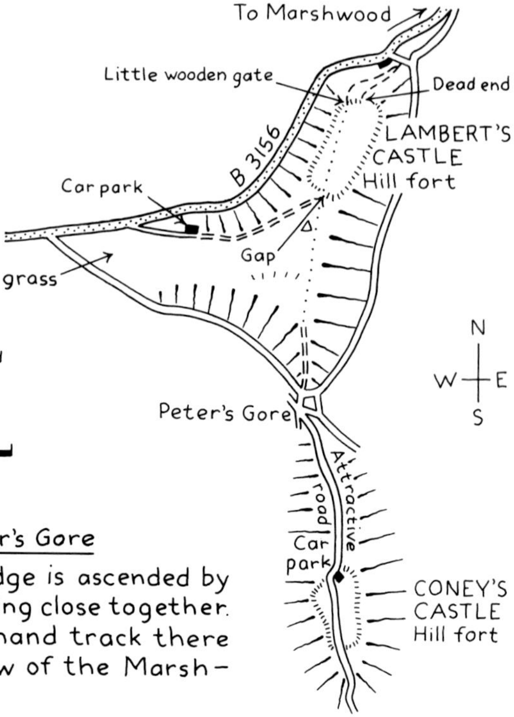

To Marshwood

Little wooden gate

Dead end

LAMBERT'S CASTLE Hill fort

B 3156

Car park

Gap

Area of purple moor grass

Crown copyright reserved

½ mile

Peter's Gore

N
W — E
S

Attractive road

Car park

CONEY'S CASTLE Hill fort

Ascent from Peter's Gore

The southern ridge is ascended by two tracks running close together. From the right-hand track there is a beautiful view of the Marsh-wood Vale.

Ascent from Marshwood

There is a good parking place on the main road. Follow the side road as far as the brow of the hill, and turn right by the National Trust sign. Two paths lead up through the wood. The upper path comes to a dead end, but the lower path, which is sunken and obviously very old, leads to a little wooden gate in a bank. This bank is the northern rampart of the hill fort, and is very small compared with the ramparts of Maiden Castle and Eggardon Hill.

Ascent from the car park

The gradient is so gentle this hardly counts as an ascent. Just follow the track along the fence.

The Summit

At one time the summit area was used as a racecourse. Now it is a public open space owned by the National Trust. The northern part is covered by an Iron Age hill fort, and the gap in the southern rampart is the original entrance to the fort.

Coney's Castle

Lambert's Castle is linked by a very attractive stretch of road to another Iron Age hill fort called Coney's Castle, which lies two miles to the south. Coney's Castle was occupied by Egbert the Great, the first King of England, in A.D. 833.

GUIDE TO LOCAL BUS ROUTES

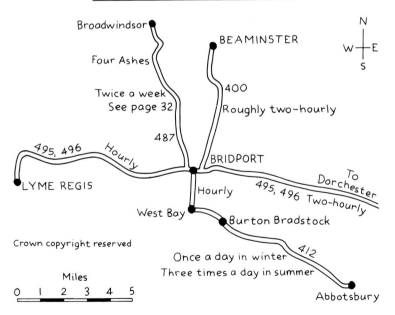

Timber Hill, Chardown Hill, Hardown Hill and Golden Cap are all close to the bus route from Bridport to Lyme Regis.

Chapter 12

PILSDON PEN

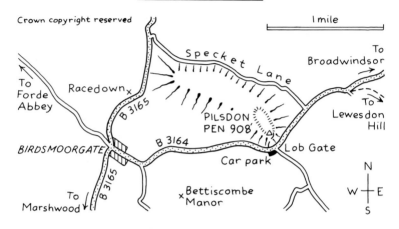

The two highest hills in Dorset, Pilsdon Pen and Lewesdon Hill, also known as the Cow and the Calf, rise to the north of the Marshwood Vale. They are about the same height, but quite different in appearance, Pilsdon Pen being crowned with an iron age hill fort, and Lewesdon Hill being covered in trees. There is a local saying "as like as Pilsdon and Lewesdon", which means "completely different".

In the vicinity of Pilsdon Pen are two houses of interest. One is Bettiscombe Manor, the home of a famous skull which is said to utter loud screams if ever it is removed from the house. The other is Racedown, where William Wordsworth lived from 1795 to 1797. It was while he was here that he first became known as a poet. In fact, it was to encourage him to write poetry that the house was provided for him. In 1797 he was joined by Samuel Taylor Coleridge.

If you take the B 3165 to the north from Birdsmoor Gate the house comes into view as you go round a right-hand bend. It is recognisable by two little round windows in the top corners.

Wordsworth climbed Pilsdon Pen many times. It was one of his favourite viewpoints.

The View

In the north the view is largely obscured by the high ground of Windwhistle Hill. It is just possible to see Wales, but this is better seen from Buckham Down. In the east the view is dominated by the bulk of Lewesdon Hill, and in the south the trees and fields of the Marshwood Vale are spread out before you like a map. The tall radio mast on the skyline in the west is the Stockland Hill I.B.A. transmitter.

Stoke Mill Farm

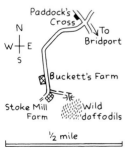

2½ miles south of Pilsdon Pen, in the heart of the Marshwood Vale, lies Stoke Mill Farm, where Dorset Knob biscuits were first made. 200 yards east of here is a place where wild daffodils grow. They are at their best in late March and early April. Just north of the farm turn left over a stile and follow the hedge. Then turn right over an attractive wooden footbridge.

Chapter 13

LEWESDON HILL

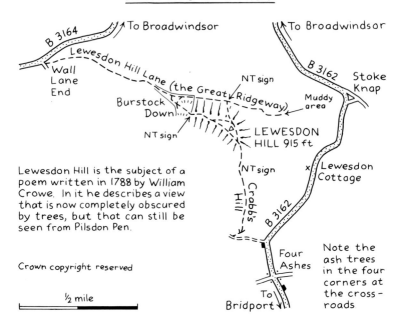

B 3164

↑ To Broadwindsor

↑ To Broadwindsor

Lewesdon Hill Lane (the Great Ridgeway)

Wall
Lane
End

NT sign

B 3162   Stoke
Knap

Burstock
Down

Muddy
area

NT sign

LEWESDON
HILL 915 ft

NT sign

x Lewesdon
Cottage

Crabb's Hill

B 3162

Four
Ashes

Note the
ash trees
in the four
corners at
the cross-
roads

To
Bridport

Lewesdon Hill is the subject of a poem written in 1788 by *William Crowe*. In it he describes a view that is now completely obscured by trees, but that can still be seen from Pilsdon Pen.

½ mile

Lewesdon Hill is served on Wednesdays and Saturdays by number 487 buses, which, at the time of writing, run at the following times:—

	Wednesdays	Saturdays
Bridport Bus Station	10·35	9·10
Four Ashes	10·55	9·30
Four Ashes	2·47	1·00
Bridport Bus Station	3·07	1·20

Chardown Hill, Hardown Hill, Golden Cap, Lambert's Castle, Pilsdon Pen and Lewesdon Hill are all capped by a layer of Greensand. This is the same rock that is found at Leith Hill in Surrey.

Ascents

The best route of ascent is from the Four Ashes, although this involves a stiff climb of 400 feet. Leave the B 3162 by a concrete road signposted to Brimley Coombe. At the top of the hill turn sharp right through a metal gate and take the second sunken path on the left. When the path leaves the gully there is a lovely view on the right. When the path becomes indistinct keep going in the same direction, passing a National Trust sign.

The route from Wall Lane End is also of interest because it follows the line of the Great Ridgeway, but it is inclined to be a little muddy in places. The path leaves the drive to Wall Farm close to its junction with the B 3164 and ascends the ridge between banks set close together. The large hole on the left is a badger sett, recognisable by the fresh earth and bedding thrown out.

Higher up the space between the banks widens out, and the path enters the bracken-covered area of Burstock Down. Here you can take a turning on the right, which leads directly to the summit, or you can go straight on and follow another interesting stretch of the old road. At the National Trust sign there is a second path to the summit, but the Ridgeway may be followed for a further quarter of a mile until it comes to an area that is exceedingly muddy.

The Summit is a wedge-shaped plateau with paths following the edges. The whole area is covered in trees, mostly beeches. From the western corner a good path follows the ridge to a subsidiary summit and a National Trust sign. The Landranger map gives the altitude of this subsidiary summit as 272 metres, but the main part of the hill appears to be considerably higher.

To settle this point I wrote to the Ordnance Survey and received a letter from Mr J. McKee saying that, according to the latest survey, the altitude of the highest point is 279 metres, or 915 feet. This means that Lewesdon Hill is the highest hill in Dorset, and that every single book that has bestowed this distinction on Pilsdon Pen is wrong.

Chapter 14

THE GREAT RIDGEWAY

The Great Ridgeway is reputed to be over 6000 years old, and is popularly regarded as the oldest road in Britain.

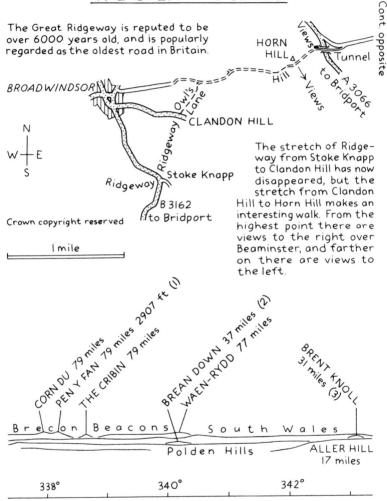

The stretch of Ridgeway from Stoke Knapp to Clandon Hill has now disappeared, but the stretch from Clandon Hill to Horn Hill makes an interesting walk. From the highest point there are views to the right over Beaminster, and farther on there are views to the left.

Crown copyright reserved

1 mile

Notes

(1) Pen y Fan is the highest point in the Brecon Beacons, and the highest point in South Wales.

(2) Brean Down is a peninsula jutting into the Bristol Channel just south of Weston-super-Mare.

(3) Brent Knoll is an isolated hill rising from the Somerset Levels.

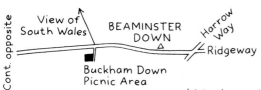

East of Horn Hill the Ridgeway follows a metalled road to Beaminster Down, where it links up with another prehistoric road, the Harrow Way. At Buckham Down there is a picnic area with views to the south that are accurately portrayed on a panorama displayed there. On a clear day you can see South Devon behind Gerard's Hill.

On a very clear day you can see the mountains of Wales through a gap in the hedge on the other side of the road. This is the view that is depicted below. Note that there is a gap between the two drawings.

Beyond Beaminster Down the Ridgeway runs along the crest of the North Dorset Downs, and continues over Cranborne Chase, Salisbury Plain, Whitehorse Hill and the Chilterns.

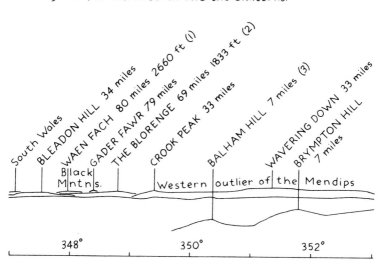

Notes

(1) Waen Fach is the highest point in the Black Mountains.

(2) The Blorenge is one of the four hills surrounding Abergavenny.

(3) Balham Hill is near Chiselborough.

Chapter 15

EGGARDON HILL

On Eggardon Hill is a very fine example of an Iron Age hill fort. Careful study has revealed that hill forts were permanently occupied towns and villages with streets and houses. The houses have long since disappeared, but their position can sometimes be made out by depressions in the ground. There are over a hundred of these hollows on Eggardon Hill.

Now the only inhabitants are the Suffolk sheep, with their black faces and legs, the skylarks, and the yellow hammers. I have also seen ravens flying over the hill, recognisable by their deep-throated croaks. Sometimes people come here for peace and quiet and to appreciate an ancient landscape. John Fowles brought Robert Robinson here on the television programme "Robinson Country"; and Nicholas Freeling's novel "The Back of the North Wind" is dedicated "To Rowland: for, among much else, taking me up Eggardon".

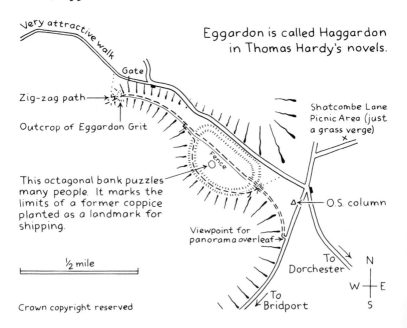

Very attractive walk

Gate

Zig-zag path →

Outcrop of Eggardon Grit

This octagonal bank puzzles many people. It marks the limits of a former coppice planted as a landmark for shipping.

½ mile

Eggardon is called Haggardon in Thomas Hardy's novels.

Shatcombe Lane Picnic Area (just a grass verge)

Fence

O.S. column

Viewpoint for panorama overleaf →

To Dorchester

To Bridport

N
W ─┼─ E
S

Ramparts on Eggardon Hill

The hill fort is approached by a level track that leaves the road by a stile 200 yards south of the Ordnance Survey column. The view from this stile is described on pages 38–39. The field on the left of the track is used for flying model aircraft.

When you reach the National Trust sign there is a choice of routes. You can go through the gate straight ahead and follow the fence across the fort to a point on the far side; or you can go through the gate on the left and follow the ramparts round to the same point. The first alternative is easier, but the second alternative is more interesting. It may be divided into three sections.

In the first section the ramparts run roughly from east to west, and the path runs along the top of the lowest rampart. On the left the hillside is covered in little terracettes, or sheep tracks, that follow the contours. Below them is an area of mixed woodland where each tree is a slightly different colour from its neighbours.

In the second section the ramparts run from south-east to north-west, but here they have been much distorted by landslips. In fact one rampart appears to have detached itself from the rest and moved down to the foot of the hill.

In the third section the ramparts run from south to north and are relatively intact. Now you can see the western spur of the hill with its outcrop of Eggardon Grit. Behind it is the village of Powerstock, and behind that are Pilsdon Pen and Lewesdon Hill.

If you follow the fence to the left you will come to

a place where you can cross it and continue along the ridge.
On the left you look down on the sweet chestnut trees
of Warren Plantation. Further west the ridge narrows.
You can keep on the path right to the end of the ridge,
or you can turn right immediately past the outcrop of
Eggardon Grit, and descend the hill by a zig-zag path.
This path is steep and slippery, and recommended only to
the young and active.

Below the zig-zag path is an interesting area of bumpy
ground scattered with boulders. Cut across this area to
an unmetalled track and turn right. Follow the track to
a metalled lane and carry straight on. After a quarter of
a mile the lane runs along the top of a rampart and makes
an exhilarating walk. This is where Gordon Beningfield
rode his bicycle in the television series "In the Country".

From the end of the lane a turning on the right leads
back to your starting point.

The View

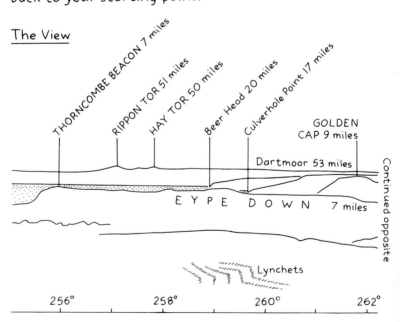

Most of these hills can be picked out on Gordon Beningfield's

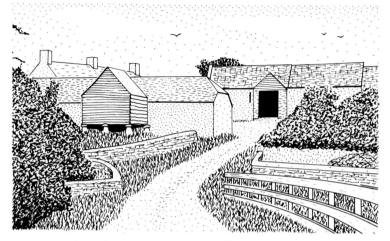

Wytherston, a typical Dorset farm,
about a mile and a half north of Eggardon

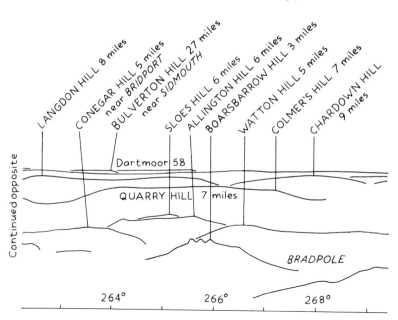

LANGDON HILL 8 miles
CONEGAR HILL 5 miles
near *BRIDPORT*
BULVERTON HILL 27 miles
near *SIDMOUTH*
SLOES HILL 6 miles
ALLINGTON HILL 6 miles
BOARSBARROW HILL 3 miles
WATTON HILL 5 miles
COLMERS HILL 7 miles
CHARDOWN HILL 9 miles

Continued opposite

Dartmoor 58

QUARRY HILL   7 miles

BRADPOLE

264°   266°   268°

painting on the cover of "The Darkling Thrush".

Chapter 16

BLACK DOWN

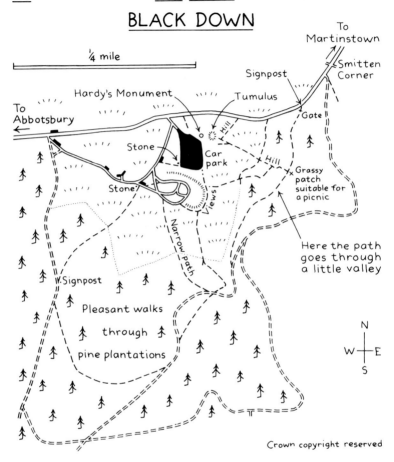

To Martinstown

Smitten Corner

Signpost

Tumulus

Hardy's Monument

To Abbotsbury

Stone

Gate

Car park

Stone

Views

Hill

Grassy patch suitable for a picnic

Narrow path

Here the path goes through a little valley

Signpost

Pleasant walks

through

pine plantations

N
W E
S

According to the Ordnance Survey it is Black Down. According to the Forestry Commission it is Blackdown (one word). Locally it is known as Blagdon, and in Hardy's books it is Black'on.

Whatever you like to call it, Black Down is the highest point on the South Dorset Downs. It lies at the junction of three ridges, one running north-west to Martin's Down, one running south-west to Abbotsbury Castle, and the third running east to White Horse Hill.

All the surrounding hills are chalk, but at Black Down the chalk is overlain by a thin layer of Bagshot Beds, so Black Down might be regarded as an outlier of the Dorset Heath. The lower slopes have now been planted with conifers, but there is still much heathland left on the top of the hill.

On the highest point is the Hardy Monument, an immense column looking rather like a factory chimney. It is visible from the birthplace of Thomas Hardy the author, and one might reasonably assume that it was erected in his memory; but one would be wrong, for the monument was erected in 1844 when the author was only four years old, and the Hardy that is commemorated here is Admiral Sir Thomas Masterman Hardy, who was flag captain to Nelson at the Battle of Trafalgar.

The Hell Stone

On the high ground to the west of Black Down are a number of prehistoric monuments. The Grey Mare and her Colts is a long barrow with two vertical stones at one end; and the Hell Stone is a cromlech with nine orthostats and a capstone. Beyond the Grey Mare and her Colts is the Kingston Russel Stone Circle, which is the subject of a poem by Michael Norman; and half a mile north-west of Portesham is the Hampton Hill Stone Circle.

The only one of these monuments that is worth visiting is the Hell Stone. Like the Heel Stone at Stonehenge it derives its name from the Celtic word "hel", meaning sun. Take the road to the west from Black Down. Turn left at the cross-roads, and park at the top of the hill. Follow the Dorset Coast Path along the fence to the left, and at the end of the first field cut across to the right. The cromlech is on the far side of a wall and hidden by a hawthorn bush. It is like a little house inside.

The view from Hardy's Monument

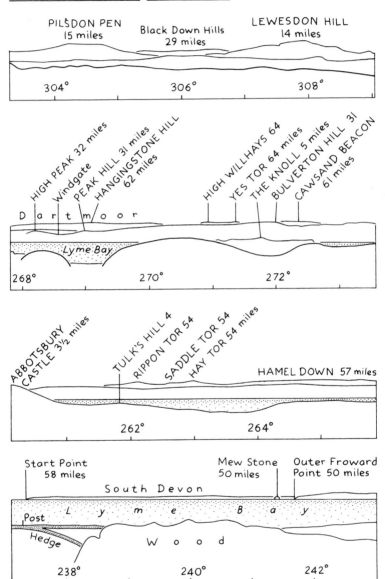

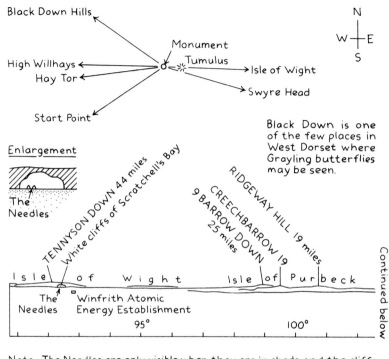

Black Down Hills

Monument
Tumulus

High Willhays ←
Hay Tor ←

→ Isle of Wight

→ Swyre Head

Start Point ←

N
W — E
S

Black Down is one of the few places in West Dorset where Grayling butterflies may be seen.

Enlargement

The Needles

TENNYSON DOWN 44 miles
White cliffs of Scratchell's Bay
RIDGEWAY HILL 19 miles
CREECHBARROW 19
BARROW DOWN 25 miles

Isle   of   Wight   Isle of Purbeck

The Needles   Winfrith Atomic Energy Establishment

95°   100°

Continued below

Note—The Needles are only visible when they are in shade and the cliffs behind them are in sun, or vice versa.

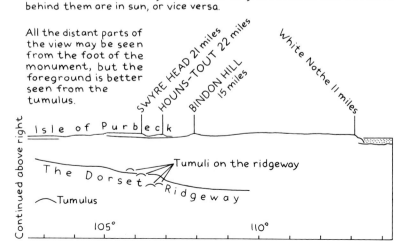

All the distant parts of the view may be seen from the foot of the monument, but the foreground is better seen from the tumulus.

SWYRE HEAD 21 miles
HOUNS-TOUT 22 miles
BINDON HILL 15 miles
White Nothe 11 miles

Continued above right

Isle of Purbeck

The Dorset Ridgeway

Tumuli on the ridgeway

Tumulus

105°   110°

Chapter 17

ABBOTSBURY

Abbotsbury is remarkable for three things:—

(1) the survival of a whole village from the seventeenth and eighteenth centuries

(2) the survival of a handful of buildings from the fourteenth century

(3) the survival of the ancient custom of Garland Day on the nearest Saturday to May 13th, when the children of the village collect garlands of flowers to be cast into the sea.

The Ordnance Survey shows an abbey in Abbotsbury (even on the Routemaster map), but there is so little of it left very few people ever find it, unless they happen to trip over it.

Abbotsbury is called
Abbotsea in Thomas
Hardy's novels.

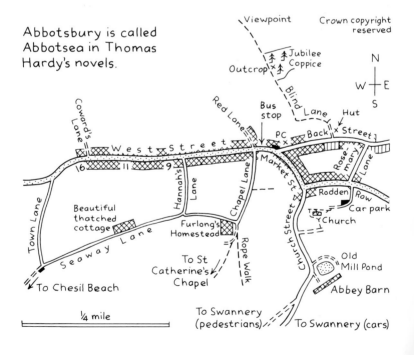

A walk round the village

Leave the car park by an unmetalled road between walls. Turn left through a kissing gate into the churchyard. The path turns sharp right and forks. From here you can see the top of the fourteenth-century windows of the Abbot's Parlour, now a house called Abbot's Walk.

Take the right fork, passing to the right of the church. In the churchyard, opposite the porch, are two mediaeval stone coffins. Inside the porch is a twelfth-century statue of an abbot carrying a book.

Keep straight on along a paved path, then turn left into another path which goes past the church tower. Above the entrance is a window, and above this window is the oldest part of the church, a small Saxon carving of a seated man with an even smaller figure between his feet.

Just before the path bends left, leave it by an unsurfaced path. Close to the junction is all that remains of St Peter's Abbey—the foundations of a short stretch of fifteenth-century wall.

The path comes out into Abbey Green. In front of you is the ruin called Pynion End, built in about 1400, with a fireplace on the ground floor. To the left of it is Abbey House.

Turn right here, passing under a seventeenth-century stone archway, and turn left into Church Street. On the right is the fourteenth-century Abbey Dairy House. This was originally the Inner Gatehouse. The huge blocked archway facing the road was the entrance for carriages. The smaller archway to the right of it was the pedestrian entrance, or postern. The window above the postern is original, and so are the buttresses supporting the side wall.

Straight ahead of you is the celebrated Abbey Barn, the longest tithe barn in Britain, and a magnificent piece of architecture. It was built in about 1400, and is 272 feet long. Half of it is roofed, and half is open to the sky. The roofed part is used to store reeds for thatching. From a gap in the wall at the far end of the unroofed part you can see the mediaeval dovecote standing on its own in a field. The dormer windows are new, but the two doorways on the ground floor are old.

Adjoining the barn to the north is the Old Mill Pond, and beyond it is the mediaeval granary, distinguishable by two little arches at ground level. It can be seen across the pond from the barn, but it is better seen from the track that skirts the pond to the north.

To see the rest of the village, retrace your steps along Church Street, but instead of turning right under the seventeenth-century archway, keep straight on, passing through the remains of the Outer Gateway. Opposite the entrance to the church is the Old Manor House, a sixteenth-century building of great charm. On the side wall of the adjoining house is a blocked 14th-century window which is entirely hidden by vegetation. On the other side of the road there are house martins' nests under the eaves.

Go straight on at the junction into Market Street, and continue into West Street, which is consistently attractive throughout its length. Several of the houses (numbers 9, 15 and 16) incorporate carved stone-work from the abbey, and one (number 11) has a Saxon carved stone head over one of its windows. This is the oldest feature in the village.

The other streets—Rodden Row, Rosemary Lane and Back Street—are equally attractive; and Blind Lane is an old road that has now become a footpath. It leaves Back Street by the basket maker's hut and climbs the hillside above the village. At Jubilee Coppice there is an outcrop of Abbotsbury Iron Ore with bands of iron running in all directions. Higher up there is a beautiful view of Abbotsbury with the Fleet behind it.

Abbotsbury Swannery

The Swannery is the oldest and largest in Britain. It is situated at the head of the Fleet, where the tidal range and salinity are very much less than in the open sea. It is open to the public from May to September. The best time to come is in May and June, when there are eggs and cygnets. John Fair the Swanherd is very knowledgeable, and will stop and talk to visitors. There has been a swanherd here since 1393.

The Swannery car park is situated on the road to the south from Abbotsbury, a quarter of a mile past the tithe barn. You can walk from the car park to the Swannery, or you can ride in a horse-drawn wagonette and miss the notices about the withy bed and the pond. Just inside the gate on the left is a pole twenty-two feet high indicating the height of the tide on November 23rd, 1824. From here a streamside path leads down to the rearing pens. There are about six hundred swans here altogether.

Abbotsbury Gardens

It makes a refreshing change to leave the Dorset countryside with its oaks and beeches and sycamores, and come to a place where most of the trees are un-familiar: where there are Japanese cedars, cork oaks and Monterey pines, and where many of the trees and plants are labelled for identification.

Peacocks roam the grounds making weird noises, and close to the tea room there is an aviary with zebra finches and other beautiful little birds. On the far side of the Lower Pond, next to where the paths fork, is an oak tree 135 feet high. This is equal in height to the tallest Common Oak in Britain.

To get to the gardens, take the Bridport road out of Abbotsbury, and bear left at the end of the village. They are open daily from 10 a.m. to 6 p.m. from the middle of March until the middle of October.

Chapel Hill Walk

In the vicinity of Abbotsbury there are three waymarked walks which were first set out in 1985. They all return to their starting points, and they all contain stretches of interest. The best of these is Chapel Hill Walk, which is defined by black triangles. It is 1½ miles long, with 250 feet of ascent and descent.

Leave the main street by Chapel Lane, an attractive unmetalled road. Halfway along on the left is a walled path. This path, and the second half of Chapel Lane, mark the western limits of the former Abbey Precinct. On the left is the field called Broad Garden, which is often grazed by shire horses.

When the lane bends right, go straight on through a gate and bear right along a track. On the right is a group of farm buildings with the lovely name of Furlong's Homestead. The goats in the farmyard are Toggenburgs, and supply milk which is sold in the village. When the track curves right, aim for the black railings in the corner of the field straight ahead.

The drawings below show the historic buildings of Abbotsbury as seen from the railings.

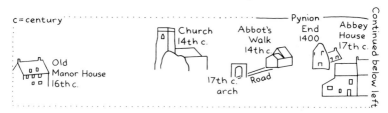

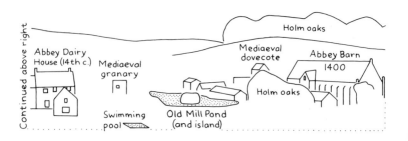

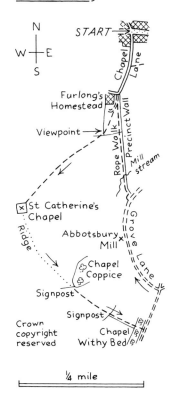

N
W —+— E
S

START

Chapel Lane

Furlong's Homestead

Viewpoint

Rope Walk

Precinct Wall

Mill stream

St Catherine's Chapel

Ridge

Abbotsbury Mill

Chapel Coppice

Lane

Signpost

Signpost

Crown copyright reserved

Chapel Withy Bed

¼ mile

Go through the kissing gates and climb the hill to St Catherine's Chapel. The chapel was built in the fourteenth century, and has walls four feet thick supported on all sides by massive buttresses. It was clearly intended to last for centuries, and it has done so.

To the left of the chapel is a signpost with a black triangle on it, but this points a little too far to the left. To find the next signpost, walk along the ridge, and then aim for the right-hand end of Chapel Coppice.

Follow the signposts down the hill, through the Chapel Withy Bed and over the stream. On the right is a notice board with information about the withy bed.

Turn left into an unmetalled road, and left again at the crossroads into Grove Lane. In 200 yards you pass a building with a round-headed window on the ground floor. This was formerly Abbotsbury Mill. The mill race emerges from a stone archway, and there is a millstone leaning against the wall to the right of the gate.

Continue along a short stretch of typical country lane, and turn left over a stile marked with a black triangle. Pass under a magnificent plane tree with great spreading branches, and follow the broad grassy path called the Rope Walk along the side of the Precinct Wall. Cross over the mill stream, and note how it has been diverted to one side of the valley in order to build up a head of water. The path eventually leads back to Chapel Lane, where the walk began.

The Lime Kiln Walk is of interest because it links up two attractive stretches of disused mediaeval road. It is marked by black squares, and is 2½ miles long, with 250 feet of ascent and descent.

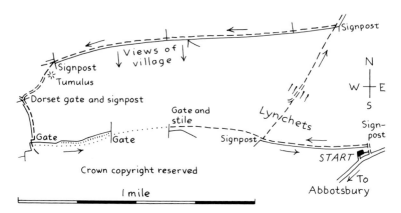

From Market Street turn into Back Street, and keep straight on for ¾ mile to the Bishop's Limekiln Picnic Area, where the walk begins. There is a notice board here with information about the lime kiln. Leave the car park by a short path that runs parallel with the road. Turn left onto a track, and then left again onto a signposted path running along the hillside parallel with the fence.

In a quarter of a mile turn sharp right onto a signposted path that follows the course of the mediaeval road from Abbotsbury to Cerne Abbas. It doesn't go straight up the hill, but inclines slightly to the right. Note that the lynchets on the left are at a different level from those on the right, indicating that the road is older than the lynchets. All the slopes in this area are accurately depicted on the Pathfinder map.

At the steepest part of the hill the old road is clearly discernable as a sunken grassy ride, but when the ground levels out the road becomes difficult to follow. Keep going in the same direction until you come to the next signpost, then turn sharp left. Keep straight on for ¾ mile, then follow another signpost diagonally downhill, passing to the right of a tumulus. The route now follows an attractive track along the slope, with outcropping rocks near by. This is part of the mediaeval road from Abbotsbury to Long Bredy via Gorwell Farm. The lane to the south from Long Bredy is still called Abbotsbury Lane.

At the next signpost pass through a fine Dorset gate, and continue downhill. Go through another gate, then turn left, and keep on a level course all the way back to the car park.

The Hill Fort Walk includes the best route for walkers from Abbotsbury to the sea, and a ridge walk over the hill fort of Abbotsbury Castle that is sheer delight; but the uninteresting uphill stretch through East Bexington Farm, and particularly the steep and muddy climb through the brambles of Tulk's Hill, make the walk as a whole not worth doing.

To walk to the sea from Abbotsbury go along Chapel Lane and follow it round to the right. Then keep going straight on. In three quarters of a mile the track becomes a path, and there are tamarisk bushes growing on the right-hand side. The beach is described on page 27.

Abbotsbury Castle

The hill fort may be reached from the B 3157 by taking the road signposted to Ashley Chase. There is a small car park on the left over the brow of the hill. From here there are very enjoyable walks in both directions. That to the west goes over the ramparts to the Ordnance Survey column, and that to the east follows the crest of a narrow ridge to a tumulus. Beyond the tumulus the ridge widens out and the walk becomes less interesting.

The layby at the top of Abbotsbury Hill is the classic viewpoint for Chesil Beach and the Fleet.

HOUSES AND GARDENS OPEN TO THE PUBLIC

<u>Parnham House</u> is situated half a mile south of Beaminster on the Bridport road. It is open on Wednesdays, Sundays and Bank Holidays from 10·0 a.m. to 5·0 p.m. from April to October.

Parnham House is a Grade I listed building of considerable architectural merit, and was chosen to illustrate the cover of the 1983 edition of "Historic Houses, Castles and Gardens". In 1976 it became the home of the John Makepiece Furniture Workshop and the School for Craftsmen in Wood. As a result the house is a curious mixture of the very old and the very new. The Great Hall, with its screens passage and minstrels' gallery, is mediaeval in character, but all the furniture is modern, most of it having been made on the premises.

In the grounds are enormous statues of Eric Morecambe and Ernie Wise.

Mapperton Manor

Take the A 3066 from Bridport to Beaminster, and turn right at Melplash church; or take the B 3163 from Beaminster to Evershot and turn right in about a mile. The house is not open, but the gardens are open from 2.0 p.m. to 6.0 p.m. from Monday to Friday.

Turn off the road, drive past the front of the house and park under the horse chestnut trees, then walk back the way you came, along the drive. On the left is a court-yard with seventeenth-century outbuildings either side of it. On the right is the best part of the house, the west front. Go in through the gate and turn left. Then turn right along the side of the house and follow the path round to the right. If you stand at the top of the steps you can see how a natural valley has been transformed into a secluded formal garden. There are more beautiful gardens than this, but is there any that blends so harmoniously with its surroundings?

Abbotsbury Gardens See page 47.

Forde Abbey

Forde Abbey is not an abbey, but an enormous country house. It is signposted from the junction of the B 3164 and B 3165 three miles west of Broadwindsor, and is open to the public from 2 p.m. to 6 p.m. on Wednesdays, Sundays and Bank Holiday Mondays from May to September.

Most of the house was built in the sixteenth and seven-teenth centuries, but there are parts surviving from the fifteenth and thirteenth centuries, and in the chapel there are cussion capitals and chevron mouldings from the twelfth century.

The part of the house facing the car park is the Dorter Range, with the Chapel on the left. The four-light window directly below the gable is that of the Bentham Room. Jeremy Bentham the philosopher lived in Forde Abbey from 1815 to 1818, and this is believed to have been his bedroom.

Continued overleaf

To reach the entrance, go to the left of the chapel and pass a row of attractive traceried windows. The one on the right was made in wood to imitate the stonework.

The entrance porch forms the ground floor of Chard's Tower, a three-storey sixteenth-century structure with richly-carved stonework. To the left of the tower is the Great Hall of the same period, and to the right of the tower, on the first floor, is the 17th-century Saloon.

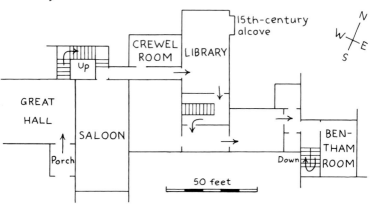

From the porch you enter the Great Hall, and ascend by the Grand Staircase to the Saloon, a sumptuous high-ceilinged room once used as a workroom by Jeremy Bentham and John Stuart Mill. I prefer the room on the other side of the corridor, the Crewel Room, which is smaller and less luxurious, with a fifteenth-century roof and a four-poster bed.

Another room with a fifteenth-century roof is the Library, which is at the end of the corridor. The alcove in the far corner of the room also dates from this period.

From the Library, the route passes through a succession of south-facing rooms and descends to the ground floor. Here you enter one of the most attractive parts of the house, the Cloister, its weathered stonework enhanced by asparagus plants. Halfway along two panels have been removed from the sixteenth-century arcading revealing the thirteenth-century arcading behind it.

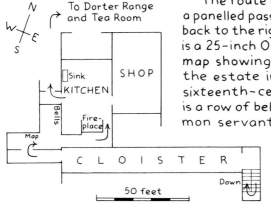

The route continues along a panelled passage and doubles back to the right. On the wall is a 25-inch Ordnance Survey map showing the extent of the estate in 1964. Above a sixteenth-century archway is a row of bells used to summon servants and bearing the names of 22 rooms. The complicated nature of this part of the house reflects the many alterations that have been made over the centuries.

The passage leads eventually to the kitchen. On your left as you enter the room is a fifteenth-century fireplace. On your right is the entrance to the shop. On the other side of the room is a large fifteenth-century window with a wooden sink beneath it. Through this window is a view of an interesting corner of the house.

Leave the kitchen by the door to the left of this window, and turn right. As you leave the house, look across to the right at the Dorter Range. Low down on the left is the relieving arch of a former watercourse, and on the first floor are thirteen narrow thirteenth-century windows. The mediaeval Undercroft is now used as a tea room.

In the grounds there is a string of lakes, the Long Pond, the Mermaid Pond, the Canal Pond and the Great Pond. At the lower end of the Great Pond is a beech hedge in the form of a house complete with roof, doorways and a window overlooking the lake. The last time I was there I saw a grass snake swimming in the Mermaid Pond.

A DRIVE THROUGH THE LANES OF WEST DORSET

This 25-mile drive has been designed to link up some of the most attractive lanes and villages in the area to the east of Bridport.

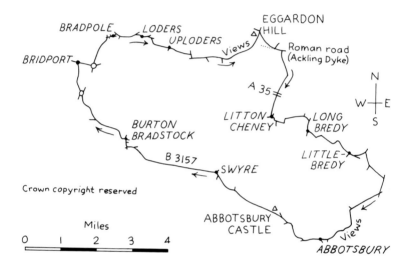

From the centre of Bridport take the Dorchester road, and turn left at the roundabout onto the A 3066. In about a mile turn right by the King's Head to Bradpole. Ignore a turning on the left. Bear left at the fork, and turn right at the T-junction.

In half a mile you pass the sunken lane called Yellow Lane and enter the village of Loders. This is a typical Dorset village, with mellow stone cottages on both sides of the road. Halfway along there is a glimpse of the village pound on the left. Follow the road round to the right, and keep straight on through the village of Uploders. Just past the sign saying Upton Manor Farmhouse there is a view on the left of an idyllic farmyard scene.

Follow the road round to the right, and then left, and keep straight on to the top of the hill. Just past the sign saying "single track road" is a passing place on the left. This is one of my favourite spots. In front of you are the ramparts of Eggardon Hill, and on your left is a view over an enchanting landscape of woods and fields and farms. The uneven nature of the ground is due to landslips.

Go over the brow of the hill, and turn sharp right at the cross-roads. In half a mile the road bends slightly left to join the line of the Roman road, which continues to the west as a hedge. Ignore a turning on the left, and turn right by three radio masts. As you pass the third mast, a small nick in the skyline ahead indicates the position of Abbotsbury Castle.

In about a mile you come to a dual carriageway. Go straight on, and descend the lane called the Whiteway into the beautiful village of Litton Cheney. The lane acquired its name before it was surfaced, when the bare chalk was exposed. Turn left in the village, and, in two hundred yards, follow the road round to the left. On the left is a barn built of chalk. Past it is an attractive thatched wall and beyond that a garden door with the date 1719 over it.

At the brow of the hill go straight on. Then follow the road round to the right into the village of Long Bredy, where a clear stream flows along the side of the road.

In a quarter of a mile turn left into a road that follows the upper part of the Bride Valley to Littlebredy. Bear left at the phone box, and turn right at the top of the hill. Hardy's Monument is now visible on the left. Ignore a turning on the right. When the end of the road is in sight you can see on the right the highest part of the Bride Valley, the Valley of Stones.

Turn right at the T-junction, and right again at the cross-roads. In about a mile there is a good view on the left down a valley to the Isle of Portland. The road bends left by a Dorset gate and descends to Abbotsbury by a long hill characterised by glorious views and masses of wild flowers. Every July there are pyramidal orchids in bloom along the grass verges.

In Abbotsbury bear right, and then right again onto the B 3157. At the top of the hill on the right is the hill-fort of Abbotsbury Castle. A little farther on the road emerges from a cutting and yet another glorious vista opens up ahead.

The road you are on leads back to Bridport, but before you get there it would be a good idea to stop and walk round Burton Bradstock, which is the most beautiful village in West Dorset apart from Abbotsbury.

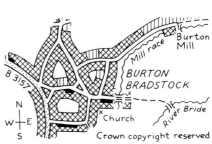

SOME WEST DORSET VILLAGES

<u>Symondsbury</u> is approached by a country lane a mile to the west of Bridport. Paul Nash came here to paint, and at one time William Barnes lived in the rectory.

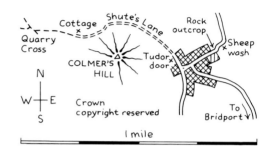

A quarter of a mile from Symondsbury is Colmer's Hill, whose symmetrical outline, capped by a clump of trees, has been adopted as a trade mark by the Dorset Craft Guild. The trees were planted to celebrate the 21st birthday of Sir Philip Colfox.

Skirting the hill to the north is Shute's Lane, a lane so old that it has been worn down by the passage of feet to form a deep gorge. The best part is beyond the cottage.

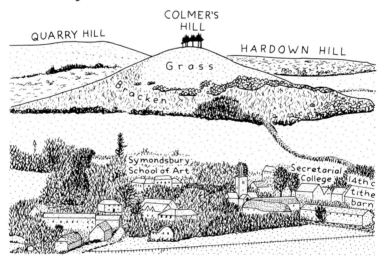

Symondsbury and Colmer's Hill as seen from Allington Hill

Powerstock

Powerstock was used as the location for the television serial "A Murder is Announced", broadcast early in 1985. A quarter of a mile to the east is Powerstock Castle, a Norman motte and bailey built on the site of a palace of King Athelstan and later used as a hunting lodge by King John.

Littlebredy has many thatched cottages with diamond-leaded windows. Three features of the village have been made Countryside Treasures —the path to the church (Church Walk), the little River Bride, with its clear sparkling water, and Bridehead Lake. The lake never freezes, but in very cold weather the spray from the waterfall collects on blades of grass and produces some exquisite pieces of ice sculpture. Near by is a fine Japanese cedar.

Crown copyright reserved

Other villages that are worth exploring are Chideock, Bothenhampton, Shipton Gorge, Stoke Abbott, Netherbury, West Milton, Loders, Askerswell, Litton Cheney, Long Bredy and Puncknowle.

INDEX

Page numbers underlined refer to illustrations.

Page numbers in brackets refer to maps.

Other page numbers refer to the text.

Figures after the decimal point indicate the approximate position on the page (from 1 at the top down to 9 at the bottom).

Postscript

On February 25th 1986, after three weeks of cold weather, we went to Bridehead to see if the ice formations were as good as they were last year. On the way there we saw a snipe fly up out of the road. At Littlebredy we sat in the car and watched the birds. Everywhere we looked there were lapwings, redwings and field-fares. Just as we were about to leave we saw a fox running across the hillside. In the River Bride we saw a large brown trout, and on the way home we saw two deer running across a field at the foot of Eggardon Hill.

Even in the depth of winter there is plenty to see in the West Dorset countryside.